OVERCOMING THE ODDS: A YOUNG WOMAN'S STRUGGLES TO STRENGTH

Hey Ms Murphy!
I pray this book blesses
you. Romans 8:28
Love you
Kourtney

The fear of the LORD is the beginning

of wisdom and knowledge of the

Holy One is understanding.

- Proverbs 9:10

OVERCOMING THE ODDS:
A YOUNG WOMAN'S STRUGGLES
TO STRENGTH

By Kourtney Renee Greene

"There is no fear in love; but perfect love casteth out fear: because fear hath torment. He that feareth is not made perfect in love"
-1 John 4:18

"Scriptures taken from both the New King James and the NIV Bible versions. New King James, Copyright © 1982 by Thomas Nelson, Inc. Used by permission. All rights reserved." Scripture taken from The Holy Bible, New International Version NIV* Copyright 1973, 1978, and 1984 by International Bible Society, used by permission. Carlyle Books does not assume any responsibility or liability for any content of this book, as the company only contracts to design and print this and all other books. All rights reserved worldwide. All other quotes are owned by the names of the authors listed after each such quote. Cover designed by Brandon Crowder.

Library of Congress Cataloging in Publication Data
Kourtney Renee Greene

OVERCOMING THE ODDS:
A YOUNG WOMAN'S STRUGGLES
TO STRENGTH

Christianity/Inspiration In Life/LifeReligious Aspects. 2. Success-Bliss, Religious Aspects. 3. Greene, Kourtney Renee.

Visit my website at:
www.wix.com/prophetessk/pk

First Edition: March 2011
Printed in the U.S.A.

Put on the full armor of God so that you can take your stand against the devil's schemes. - Ephesians 6:11

"The LORD God is my strength, and he will make my feet like hinds' feet, and he will make me to walk upon mine high places." Habakkuk 3:19

CONTENTS

Foreword: By Donna James   13

Introduction: Childhood Pain, Head Start & First Grade 17

CHAPTER 1 A Lesson Learned—High School   29

CHAPTER 2 The Manifestation   37

CHAPTER 3 Moving Out   45

CHAPTER 4 Moving Day   59

CHAPTER 5 Unbreakable   67

CHAPTER 6 Way Of Escape   75

CHAPTER 7 Transition   80

CHAPTER 8 Overcoming The Odds   87

Preface: Sleep'n with the Enemy

About the Author

"Thou rulest the raging sea; when the waves thereof arise, thou stillest them."
-Psalm 89:9

OVERCOMING THE ODDS: A YOUNG WOMAN'S STRUGGLES TO STRENGTH

Inspirational Autobiography Novel
Foreword: By Donna James

When a child is born, it takes that first breath; scared of the unknown but seeking what is familiar. Strange hands work to clean and swaddle it in order to calm and help the baby feel connected like in the womb.

This book is about the struggle of a young lady to feel connected to someone or something. Like a newborn, she starts off trusting those who have been placed in positions to read her emotions and body language and respond accordingly. Responses that should have helped mold her and make her feel welcomed, loved, stimulated, and appreciated instead lowered her self esteem and temporarily stunted her growth. I was honored to meet this young lady, at a time in her life when a wrong move would have caused her to shatter like glass.

If this is not your story, then you know of someone who has visited similar pivotal points in their life that has either broken them or given them a reason to push forward. Ms. Greene has used her past as a stepping stone into her tomorrow. With each forced step, she stumbled but refused to give up. At times when she could not see, feel, or hear the one calling her, she forced herself to keep moving; never giving up hope.

Kourtney Greene has opened the door to her heart, exposing all so that it may be a blessing to someone else that has gone or is going through the darkness of life. I would like to thank Ms. Greene for following her calling and using her gift of gab. She is a true blessing to all who crosses her path.

I can do all things through Christ, because he gives me strength. Philippians 4:13

"The LORD is good, a refuge in times of trouble.
He cares for those who trust in Him"
-Nahum 1:7

"Submit yourselves unto to God, resist the devil
and he shall flee." James 4:7

"But the fruit of the Spirit is love, joy, peace,

patience, kindness, goodness, faithfulness,

gentleness and self-control." -Galatians 5: 22-23

INTRODUCTION
CHILDHOOD PAIN

"The Bows of the mighty men are broken and those who stumbled are girded up with strength." (1 Samuel 2:4)

This autobiography tells of the accounts of abuse I experienced throughout the course of my life. What was meant to break me became my strength and testimony to overcome any situation and circumstance that came my way.

This book is centered around the odds, of me trying to graduate from high school and not fall into the statistics of life. This book starts off with my first encounter of abuse at the age of four on throughout my life until I graduated from high school. This book is to help encourage, and empower those who have been bound by abuse, to come out and be free.

I would like to give a special thanks to my Lord and Savior for waking me up every day to write this book. I also would like to give thanks to my mother for being behind me 100% when it came to actually getting the book done. Thanks Derrick for staying up with me for hours hundreds of miles away seeing the vision with me and pushing me.

To all of those people who put up with me, both family and friends during my walk to Christ, thanks for the criticism. It has helped mold me into the Woman of God I have been called to be. Also, I would like to thank a mighty man of God who helped produce the cover God desired for this book Mr. Crowder, may God continue to enlarge and increase your territory. Lastly, I would like to give thanks to Don Williams, and his production team, you have truly been a great help with the vision of this book, and publishing.

I decree a special blessing over everyone who gets this book in their hands, may this book be used to help edify and build God's kingdom.

"The LORD will keep you from all harm—he will watch over your life; the LORD will watch over your coming and going both now and forevermore." -Psalm 121:7-8

HEAD START

About to burst with excitement I trotted into the classroom, ready to take my school pictures. While waiting to be called the teacher passed out the little black combs every child gets just in case they mess up their hair.

While I was sitting at my desk a young man named Courtney sat next to me, laid his head on the desk, and stared. I smiled cordially, and then my name was called so I got up and made my way to the hallway.

After taking my pictures I went out to the playground and stood against the wall. I didn't dare go join the other kids I refused to mess up my new dress.

Courtney walked out the door and made his way over to me. When he came to me, he stood in front of me and put his arms around me. Next, he took his hand and slid it up my skirt. I remembered telling him to stop but he wouldn't, he kept trying to stick his hands inside my panties.

After I started crying he stopped and left me alone. I felt scarred. After that happened, I begun to get angry and would avoid him every chance I got. After that day I never wanted to wear another skirt as long as I lived. Little did I know, this would be the start of an era of abuse that I would experience for the next 14 years.

"For the weapons of our warfare are
not carnal." 2 Corinthians 10:4

**Scripture says, "My people
shall perish for lack of wisdom!"**

FIRST GRADE

When I was 5 years old our family moved to Decatur, Illinois. While my mom worked I had a horrible lazy babysitter named Ms. Tina. Ms. Tina was getting paid by the state to lie in her bed, watch soap operas, and the Price is Right everyday. My first day there I met this boy named Daniel. 'He would always follow me.'

Every time he got a chance to be alone with me he would try to grind on me. It got to a point where I no longer enjoyed going to Ms. Tina's house. Daniel had a habit of pulling me behind the couch onto the floor. I was so tired of him doing it, but I never said a word to anyone. I just accepted it for what it was. No woman or man should feel like its ok to be touched, or abused in anyway. Those acts of abuse are very detrimental to a person's mind and spirit. Although, I didn't realize it at the time, the next series of abuse catapulted me to a personal relationship with God.

1 My son, do not forget my teaching,
but keep my commands in your heart,
2 for they will prolong your life many years
and bring you prosperity.
3 Let love and faithfulness never leave you;
bind them around your neck,
write them on the tablet of your heart.
4 Then you will win favor and a good name
in the sight of God and man.
5 Trust in the Lord with all your heart
and lean not on your own understanding;
6 in all your ways acknowledge him,
and he will make your paths straight.
7 Do not be wise in your own eyes;
fear the Lord and shun evil.
8 This will bring health to your body
and nourishment to your bones.

PROVERBS 3:1-8

All great achievements require time.
-Maya Angelou

CHAPTER ONE

A LESSON LEARNED
HIGH SCHOOL

At the age of 16, I met my first love: John. During the course of our relationship we had a lot of issues. His mother who was raised in a family where blacks used to work for them, and my mother coming from a family who didn't associate themselves with whites shunned our love. I remember right before our six month anniversary every girl who was in a relationship was wearing promise rings. I told John for months that on our six month anniversary I wanted a pretty ring like the others. He assured me that he would give me whatever my heart desired.

On our anniversary John came to school with a large dog he had won the night before at the fair, and a ring. I was elated not about the dog, but about the ring. He told me to close my eyes so he could put the ring on my finger.

It felt a little snug, as I opened my eyes slowly and looked down it was plastic! I had mixed emotions of hurt, frustration, and anger. He looked at me with the dumbest look on his face. He had the audacity to laugh and say I got it out of the quarter machine. Out of anger I took it off and threw it at him. I felt like he failed me and from that day forth our relationship went downhill, until we eventually broke up. I vowed I would never date again.

Boy was I wrong. A few months later I stayed after school one day. I ran into this guy named James, he called himself trying to hit on me and, I fell for it. James happened to be the little brother of one of my best guy friends. James was an all American sports kid, who was well-known on the high school football team. The relationship we had was crazy. I started noticing that he had a lot of issues. He drank a lot and developed an anger problem. While hanging out at night we would drive around, go to car lots with bats and he would bust the windows out of the cars. Some nights we would drive around while he hung out the passenger window beating the taillights and rearview mirrors on parked cars.

One particular night we saw a pedestrian riding his bike down the street. James thought it would be a great idea to jump him. So, he had one of the boys drive up next to him and he punched the man in his jaw so he would fall off his bike. After doing so he got out the car and kicked him repeatedly laughing and spitting on him. I knew something was wrong with him but I didn't leave him I stayed with him.

On Christmas day after hanging out, he decided to take me home early. He was going to surprise me with a necklace that he had gotten me as a Christmas gift (later I found out that he had stolen it). Instead of taking me home the usual way, he took another route.

> "No weapon that is formed against thee shall prosper; and every tongue that shall rise against thee in judgment thou shalt condemn," Isaiah 54:17

I kept asking him where he was taking me, but he never said a word. He parked the car on a street where there was only one streetlight and he looked at me and said, "You knew this was eventually going to happen, you've been flirting with me the whole time we've been together." He didn't kiss me or anything. He just climbed over into the passenger seat, unbuckled my pants and slid them down.

During the course of him doing this, I told him I didn't want to have sex with him, but he kept a fixated look of no emotion and wouldn't utter a word. He lifted the latch on the side of my seat to make the seat drop back, and then he proceeded to climb on top of me. In my mind I was thinking, man this is how he really feels about me, man was I really flirting with him like that, did I show signs of wanting to have sex with him?

I began telling myself, "Kourtney, you deserve this, look at you, you're not going to be nothing but a hoe. You might as well let him do it, but then I told myself this isn't right, he doesn't respect you and of all things he's doing it in a car." He reached in his pocket and pulled out a condom to put it on I could never tell if he got inside me or not. It kept feeling like a finger was poking me over and over again. I just laid there with no pleasure, and no emotion.

After what felt like an hour of being poked he got up and I pulled up my clothes feeling dirty and misused. I pulled my knees up to my chest and I leaned on the car door; crying. I felt so used, and hurt. As he drove me home he kept asking me what was wrong, and I kept crying softly to myself. It hurt how he could not see how I felt. He had no respect for me.

"Why are you crying? What's wrong with you? I'm your boyfriend; you act like it was wrong what I did. You kept flirting with me so you knew I was going to try." When I got home I had to wait on my mom because she had gone to bible study. While waiting he kept saying over and over again, "wipe your face, clean it up your mom doesn't need to know about what happened, you're going to get me into trouble."

When she pulled up I quickly wiped my face, and got out of the car. That night he called and apologized for what he had done to me. He said that he didn't mean to hurt me. The next day he and his brother picked me up for school. The whole time in the car he did not speak to me. When we got to school usually he would hug on me or hold my hand, but he did nothing. Towards the end of the day he gives me a note, and it said, "Kourtney, I don't want to be with you no more, it's just not going to work out between me and you.

We can be cool, but not together." Talk about someone hurt, confused, and frustrated, I bawled my eyes out for the rest of the day. I couldn't believe it; I felt like a toilet, I felt so hurt and dismayed. As I was leaving school that day, I walked outside and saw him hugged up with another girl. She looked like a tramp, and she resembled a redheaded leprechaun. As it turns out a couple weeks prior to us breaking up, while I was out of town visiting with my uncle he had made out with this girl. I guess it was only a matter of time before he schemed on how to break up with me.

That raised a whole new level of anger in me that I didn't know I had. All I had in my heart and mind was vengeance to him and her. I thought to myself I should end his high school football career. All I have to do was go to the police department and file a police report on rape, and then I would just beat her face in. If you don't contain anger, it can turn into hate.

**"Faith is the substance of things hoped for
the evidence of things unseen,"
-Hebrews 11:1**

CHAPTER TWO
THE MANIFESTATION

As if nothing in my life could get any worse, life at school worked my dignity. I dreaded going to school most days, for one, I was bored with my work, and I had to see James everyday with that tall redheaded whore.

There were times when he would purposely kiss her in front of me, and hold her hand. I talked about her every chance I got and didn't care who heard or if it got back to her. One day she slipped up and called me a nigger and a dumb bitch. I was pissed to no return; in passing I told her I was going to show her what a real bitch was like.

She would never meet me to fight whenever I told her to. The more I thought about what he did to me, and what she said, the angrier I became. On this particular day, it was nice and warm outside, the bell rang as usual for lunch and I decided that I would go out.

When I went outside to leave for lunch I saw her car across the street. A malicious thought crossed my mind to slash the tires on the car her dad just purchased. After thinking about it, I realized I didn't have anything to slash her tires with, so I ran in the building and asked a young man named Carlton if he had a pocket knife. With ease he reached in his pocket and handed it to me.

I had this girl named Sammy go with me outside to watch my back. Once we had gotten across the street I started to stab the tire with the knife, but became fearful. People were constantly walking down the street from their cars, and I thought it would make a loud pop noise that would draw attention. So, instead, I dug the knife into the paint of her car just above her tire. With the first stab I felt a sense of exhilaration. I also felt a release from some of the anger she caused; so I stabbed the knife into her car again, this time on the door and I drug it all the way across the paint.

Lunch was almost over so Sammy and I ran back across the street to the cafeteria. I cleaned any residue of paint off the knife blade and handed it back to Carlton. I finally felt at peace. In my mind I told myself, "I bet she won't call me another B."

Shortly afterwards I was made out to be a liar; I made my way to class, and as I sat in Art class, I heard a loud scream in the hallway. It was her voice saying, "that little black bitch" keyed my car! I started cracking up, I may be a "little black b" but her car was messed up, plus I was innocent until proven guilty.

I went through a lot of stuff within the next few weeks because of what I did. I got called into the office I don't know how many times. The last time I went I got set up into telling the truth. When I walked in the room there was a chair sitting in the center with officials sitting around it. I felt like I was in a movie. They interrogated me and said, "You might as well tell the truth, someone already told on you." I knew they were lying but I told them anyway.

Whoever has no rule over his own spirit
is like a city broken down, without walls.
- Proverbs 25:28

My punishment was a five day suspension. I called my mom and told her what happened. She didn't say much on the phone she just told me to have my stuff ready when she got there. When I got in the car, the ride was silent until we made it a block away from the school. Before I could blink she slapped me hard in the face, and I hollered in agony.

She yelled and screamed, "What was going through your head, what, you did that over some funky tailed boy?" "I raised you better than that; I can't believe you, wait till I tell your daddy!" In my mind I thought she was making too big of a deal. So I would get F's for the days I wasn't there, and yea it looked bad on my school records, but revenge was sweet.

When my dad got home, he came in my room and told me he was going to whoop me. Now at the age of 17 I knew my dad was not about to give me a whooping, I thought I was too old and grown for that. He left out the room and to my surprise came back with a leather belt in hand. Just as he did when I was a kid he told me to pull my pants down because he wanted to hit skin.

He grabbed me by my ankles and pulled me upside down and started hitting me repeatedly not saying a word. I was angry I squirmed to get away; it felt like every time I moved he would hit harder. Finally, he let me go, but didn't stop swinging and he no longer tried to hit me on my butt. He had begun to hit me everywhere.

He hit me repeatedly on my back with the belt, my face and everywhere else there was an opening. I took my hands and placed them around my throat. I kept choking myself and rocking while he kept hitting me. I wanted him to stop, and I knew if I kept choking myself he would. It worked. I looked him in the eye and told him I hated him.

"For we walk by faith, not by sight,"
says 2 Corinthians 5:7

I knew those words would hurt them both, but I wanted them to feel my pain too. I didn't understand the principle of him whooping me the way that he did. When he was done I had a welt on my face, and all over my back. I then realized it was time to go. Without hesitation I moved out.

CHAPTER THREE
MOVING OUT

It was a Sunday morning and I had made up in my mind that it was time to go. I called Amber who was my best friend at the time. She asked her mother if I could move in with them to finish out the remainder of my high school year. The day I left, my mom told me that if I left her house this time, I could never return. That was fine by me, I hated living there, and I hated not having freedom.

While living with Amber I started noticing that her father was abusive. He was always putting her down due to her weight and hitting her. We used to sit up at night and talk about the things she would go through. One day she finally got tired and decided that she would move out. That night after everyone was sleeping; we snuck out of the house and down the gravel road, and went to town. Once we made it into town we met up with my ex- boyfriend John, he had not too long moved out of his parent's house as well. He was living in the basement of one of our friends home for a few months. We snuck in that night and hid out for half the next day.

We both knew we couldn't stay there, so we got in the car in search of another place to go. While we were searching her parents drove passed us, they had realized we snuck out the house. So we booked it, we knew if we could at least make it to the police station that we would be safe. Her little cavalier tried to out run their F-150 truck, but they caught up to us. He stopped his truck in front of our car. We knew the outcome was not going to be good. After she pulled over the car, her dad reached his hand through the window, grabbed her by her hair and pulled her out. He drug her to his truck while she kicked and screamed.

Her mom jumped in the driver seat, called me a black bitch, and told me I needed to get out of her house and to never return. When we made it to the house, she told me that I was no longer allowed to associate myself with Amber. She made me sit outside until I found a place to go.

I prayed to God as hard as I could and asked him to help me find somewhere to sleep. After calling everyone that I knew, I finally found my friend, Crystal T. She said I could move in with her and her fiancé Nick. Shortly after I moved in with Crystal T., John asked to move in also and that is when all hell broke loose.

I lived in a house where I couldn't eat and I had to pay rent. At that time I was working two jobs that were barely supporting me. So in order to make more money to pay bills and eat, I had to sell drugs.

Selling drugs was an experience in its own. I used to bag the weed up myself giving the customers less than what they asked for. Instead of putting all weed leaves I would put the residue and sticks found at the bottom of the bag.

One day this method backfired in my face. I learned quickly, you can't trick a pothead. This young man, Josh, called me for a $20 sack. I bagged his weed up as usual but instead of putting the full $20 in I put $10 worth plus some sticks and rocks from the residue. After he got home from meeting me I received a phone call in which he stated, "bitch you ripped me off, I wanted the full amount and you gave me rocks. So when I see you I'm going to f u up!" After that happened I decided no longer would I sell another bag of weed for as long as I lived.

About three weeks after this incident, I woke up one morning to a note on my door. It had a smiley face on it saying that I was being evicted and that I had two hours to get out the house. Now, just a few days prior to this my dad had put $40.00 worth of food in the house for me to eat. I was distraught and angry, with nowhere to go that night I slept in my boyfriend's car. Here I am hungry, tired, and no place to go. I called my mom in hopes that she would let me stay there for at least one night, she quickly told me no and hung up.

The things a woman would do for a man who she thought she was in love with. I would call people to see if I could stay with them, many said yes, but John couldn't come along. Being that I knew what it was like to not have any place to go I wouldn't leave him stranded by himself.

Finally, I was able to get in contact with another friend who I used to baby sit for all the time. Her name was Crystal B., and she had just moved back home with her mom from St. Louis. After discussing my situation with her mom Sarah Ann, like everyone else she said that I could move in, but John couldn't. I cried, I couldn't understand why he couldn't stay with me. I told her thank you, but I wasn't going to live there I needed him with me. She called me back and told me if we could abide by the rules we could both move in.

John and I moved into the little bedroom in the front of the house. The house was filthy, but one of the rules was to keep the house clean. I didn't see no point in doing that, it always smelled like old food, and cat pee. When you walked into the kitchen there was always cat food and cat feces all over the floor. Dried up food, and spoiled meat sat on the counter at all times. I would attempt to clean the kitchen but no sooner after that it was back filthy. I was expected to watch her children as payment for living in her house. It was hard. I fed them and made sure they were clean with the help of Sarah Ann's mom when she wasn't around.

After a while I started noticing a pattern Sarah was always disappearing. She would leave for 3 to 4 days at a time sometimes with no food left in the house to feed the kids. She was getting welfare and six hundred dollars in food stamps but due to her addiction to crack cocaine she would sell them as fast as she got them. When she did purchase food she would tell me that I couldn't eat the food and that me eating the food would be taking away from the kids. I didn't eat hardly except when I went to work at Burger King.

It was hard, I was a senior in high school and I barely went to school. Every day I would pray and ask God to help me to graduate not knowing if I would.

My boyfriend was lazy. He didn't want to work. Whenever I got paid, he would steal my money, and spend it on weed. All he did was smoke weed, drink, hang out with his friends, and sleep. Living on my own was not all it was cracked up to be. Times were hard. I didn't have soap half the time to care for my hygiene, so I would use shampoo, and conditioner to clean myself; I would steal my clothes instead of washing because I didn't have a washing machine to wash them in.

At night time I do remember that when I would wake up John would be on top of me trying to penetrate me with his dirty penis. Rejection had become my best friend. Many times when I would call my mom and ask her if I could come over to get something to eat.

Sometimes she said yes and sometimes no, but no matter what, whenever I went to her house, I had to leave immediately after I ate. Along with living in this place called hell, John was abusive. At times he would talk down to me making me feel worthless. I got punched, hit and grabbed whenever he couldn't contain his anger.

I cried almost every night, because I wanted to go home, I was unhappy with my situation. I wanted out, I talked to God every single day not knowing if he could hear me, only hoping for a change.

JESUS said, "Know what is in front of your face, and what is hidden from you will be disclosed to you. For there is thing hidden that will not be revealed."

Over The Edge

We were always in need for money. Desperate to do anything, John came up with the idea to sell his car to the junk yard for some money. He came back after about five hours with a 44oz soda, a Chinese doggy bag and a pound of weed. He had sold his car for $250 and went out to eat. I was furious! I had been starving without food and the one time he gets money he goes and gets Chinese food with his boys, and smoke weed. What happened to our relationship? What happened to I'm here for you always?

The more I thought about it the madder I got and all those years of abuse, and frustration boiled through my veins. He ran upstairs and I chased him until he got all the way to the balcony door. Then I jumped on top of him. He hit the floor abruptly and I began to beat his head into the floor repeatedly over and over again.

I choked him until his face turned purple. Crystal, her boyfriend, and one of John's friends tried to pull me off of him; but couldn't. All of a sudden the voice of the Lord spoke and said "Get up, if you don't he will die." The voice was so strong that I had no choice, but to get up. He laid on the floor, gasping for air while everyone else tried to calm me down. I knew then in my spirit that it was over between me and him.

I slid the balcony doors open and I started running. The air was cool outside and my heart was racing. With every step of my feet I felt a release. I knew then that it was time to face myself. I ran all the way to my moms' house. I cried out to my mom and told her that I was ready to get myself together. I told her that it was important for me to graduate from high school. She made the suggestion that I should call my grandmother in Kentucky and see if I could move in with her. I prayed then for God to open up a door so I could get out of the situation I was in.

I went to school that next day and talked to a counselor. I told her where I lived and who I was living with. Her face lit up, it turned out that they had been looking for this woman for a while. Sarah Ann was involved in a child abuse case at the Elementary school concerning the youngest son. The school was doing their yearly check-ups and they saw an imprint of an iron on his back. A few days prior he had been jumping up and down on his sisters' bed; Crystal had left the iron plugged in on the bed face up, when he decided to fall backwards the iron was so hot it burned him leaving an imprint on his back.

Later on that day when my counselor took me home to Crystal's house there were cop cars, a social service car, and a swat van parked outside. My counselor informed me, that it wouldn't be a good idea to stop, so we kept driving past the house. God was hearing my cries and prayers. I knew then that I had to make arrangements to find another place to stay before I went to Kentucky. I wound up getting in contact with a friend from school named Amber. She and her mother said they would be glad to let me stay with them during my transition.

After about thirty minutes I went back to the house. On the way there I came up with a story so I could finally get away from John. When I got there I told him that I was going to stay at a friend's because I was going to have to go out of town to go see my sick grandmother. He cried, and asked me why, but I had to keep telling myself, Kourtney you have to stay focused, you have to graduate. I left that house that day feeling like a huge burden was being lifted off of me, but also in sorrow, because I felt like I was leaving a part of my heart.

I thought I was in love with John. He had been there since day one but the difference between us was that he was content with living in his pain, and I was not. I knew there was more to life than just being used, and mistreated. I knew that I would become someone one day. Oftentimes in my pain I would find comfort in my mind fantasizing about a life of luxury, and peace. I promised myself I would not be another statistic. I instilled in my mind these words: "You can't do it for no one else do it for yourself, you have to graduate."

"But when the kindness and love of God our Savior appeared, he saved us, not because of righteous things we had done, but because of his mercy. He saved us through the washing of rebirth and renewal by the Holy Spirit, whom he poured out on us generously through Jesus Christ our Savior." -Titus 3:46

CHAPTER FOUR
MOVING DAY

The day I left Jackson, Mo was a rainy day. I met John at the gas station to tell him good bye for the last time, and my mom pulled me into the car and told me to buckle my seat belt. As I watched him walk back to the house that had caused me a lot of pain, I cried. During the whole two hour drive I cried and felt sorry for myself. I didn't know what was in store for me in this next transition; I just knew that I was one step closer to graduating. When we got to the bridge between Illinois and Kentucky my heart leaped, my mother told me from that day forth never let another man control my emotions the way he did.

When I got to my grandmothers I was excited! Deep inside I knew this was the best decision I could have made. I brought my bags into the house and my grandmother told me for the next couple of months I would stay in the room my sister used to live in when she lived with her. This room was painted pink. She had an old worn down futon that I was to use as my bed. The curtains were stapled to the walls so no sunlight could get in, and there was wood boards nailed to the window sill with nails sticking up, just in case you try to sneak out the house.

New Image

The next day, we went through the necessary procedures to get me into school. My first day of school was interesting; coming from an all white school it was a big culture shock, because this High School was predominantly black. A trait I picked up was wearing flowers in my hair at my previous school. It was apart of my image, I made sure I had a flower for every outfit. So many people walked up to me and asked the same question, "who you supposed to be, you from Hawaii?" They never referred to me by my name I was called "the flower girl." When my credits transferred from Jackson I actually had all that was required to graduate except for a health class. Unlike Jackson, Paducah didn't let their students graduate a semester early. I had to fill my schedule up with a lot of electives, and made sure I took Health Class.

When doing my schedule I was short one elective class so they placed me in the guidance counselor's office as an aid. Imagine my luck when I walked into the guidance counselor's office and saw a young lady that I had met a few years earlier, her name was Senchal.

I was amazed she remembered me from the eighth grade. From that day forward we got to know each other all over again, and built a great friendship.

Psalm 118:89
It is better to trust in the LORD
than to put confidence in man.

I still missed my ex-boyfriend. I didn't have anyone to talk to but a guy named Bill who I had befriended during my eighth grade year the first time I lived in Paducah. Bill was what I called a "convenient" friend. When I needed to get away from my grandmother I would call him and he would come pick me up and we would go hang out. On Christmas Eve 2005 our friendship took a turn for the worse. From the time I got into the car, parking at his house, and going into his room the atmosphere felt different. He didn't say much to me.

We sat in his room in unusual silence, he closed his phone got up and turned off the light. I made the comment that it was extremely dark and he responded with a "duh." He proceeded to tell me that I should have known the day would come that he would want to sleep with me. The same emotion I felt when James said that returned, and once again I found myself feeling hurt, frustrated, and confused.

Did I have some stamp on my forehead that said, "I'm easy come get some?" My mind reverted back to the day James took me on that dark street, and out of fear I started obeying him by taking my clothes off. Here I was sitting on his bed where we once would lay to watch movies and talk, to sleeping with him. He instructed me to get on top of him and I cried and said no. Out of rage he picked up his phone called one of his boys and said, "the flower girl ain't on shit." He told me to get up off his bed put my clothes on so he could take me home. He got up threw on his clothes and ran downstairs, I felt mistreated and angry. While I was putting on my clothes I heard him on the phone, he had called another one of his boys named Damon. He lied and told him that we had sex and it wasn't good. After getting dressed I walked outside and sat in the car in silence. Like oil to dry skin depression seeped into my spirit. Before he could park his car I opened the door and got out. That would be the last day we ever spoke and hung out as friends.

Slandered

When I got back to school from Christmas break a rumor had been started. I became the girl on the movies who walked through the hallways while people whispered and snickered. Bill told everyone he had sex with me, random guys would walk up to me and ask when could they hit it. I hated school. I finally got tired and addressed him in front of everyone. I got tired of avoiding him and listening to his laughs every time he passed me in the hallway. After lunch one day while doing his daily laugh of torment I told him to shut the f up. It felt like the world had stopped. It got quiet and suddenly I didn't care what anyone said anymore. I proceeded to ask him what he got out of torturing me with his lies. He said nothing.

Once again I asked him why he didn't tell the real story, how he tried to force me to sleep with him. I asked him why did he leave out the part him calling me a b**** for not riding him? The tables turned and he felt what I felt.

What could he say or do? His face turned red and all he could do was turn around and walk to class. Everyone resumed their routine like nothing ever happened and I didn't hear another thing about it.

> **Your enemy has come to kill, steal and destroy your life but Jesus Christ loves you He will give you beauty for ashes and will restore everything back to you just trust Him and believe. -John 10:10**

CHAPTER FIVE
Unbreakable

I started noticing, more and more everyday, a change in my grandmother's behavior. She went from being sweet, to dogging my character. She would always tell me negative things. She began walking through the house talking to herself and laughing. At first it didn't bother me, but then it started scaring me. There were times at night when I would wake up and she would be standing in the door-way of my room staring at me in darkness.

That caused me to become paranoid; I was always look-ing behind my back when I was at home. When she would get mad at her boyfriend she would come into my room and start fights with me. When she would get really angry she would threaten to shoot me with her .22. I lived in constant fear for the next 3 months.

A Change for the Worse

On this particular day I woke up to a bad feeling in the pit of my stomach. Growing up I would have these feelings from time to time. Nine times out of ten usually something unexpected was going to occur. While I was sitting in class I heard in my spirit that I was going to get into a car wreck; I believed what I heard to be true. As soon as I got out of school, my grandmother picked me up, but said she had to run to the dollar store. I told her that I had a bad feeling all day, that something was going to happen.

No sooner after we got out of the dollar store, and started backing up, a car slammed into the rear of my grandmother's car causing my neck to be jolted back and forth.

After my grandmother collected the other person's insurance information she took me to the emergency room, the doctor said I had sprained my neck and gave me a prescription of some muscle relaxers and pain killers. I went home that night stiff and in pain not knowing what tomorrow would bring. When I woke up, I woke up to an empty house my grandmother was gone and I was locked in the house.

When she got home she went to her room to unlock the door. Due to her paranoia, she would never leave her room open and she would use a skeleton key to lock and unlock her door.

I was sorting clothes getting ready to wash for school the next week. My grandmother was upset because something was going on with her insurance and her car.

My heart went out to her. I reassured her that whenever I got a settlement from the Social Security Administration for my "disability" she could have all of the checks. Why did I say that? Something clicked with her wrong and she dropped her brown purse on the floor along with her keys and ran in the room. She grabbed me and body slammed me to the floor, then she got on top of me and she begun to slam my head repeatedly into the floor over and over screaming I want you to f***ing die! Die! Die!

All I could do was shield my chest, then after doing that for about 3 minutes she switched to my chest. She started beating me with her fist repeatedly over and over again saying the same thing while I kept my arms covered over my face and chest.

I was terrified, I would muster a scream for awhile, and then I began to quote scriptures over and over, and beg for God to help me. I quoted James 4:7 "submit your selves unto God, resist the devil and he shall flee from you." The last time I said it my grandmother she got up and looked down at me and said, "If Satan says kill you I'll f***ing kill you, God can't help you." I cried profusely in fear and torment.

Lying on the floor next to me was the bottle of muscle spasm pills from the accident the day before. I opened the bottle and I poured a handful of pills in my hand. I knew then that I was going to kill myself, because after all the years of physical, emotional, sexual, and mental abuse, I was tired. There was no more reason to live. I called for God and He didn't come. I thought He hated me and He didn't love me, so who was going to love me? I took three pills and before I could take the rest my grandmother, who had been standing in the door-way unaware, snatched the rest of the pills and the bottle out of my hand and said, you didn't pay for the co-pay so you can't take the pills. I curled up in a ball and cried to myself, I wanted to get out.

My grandmother called my mother then came in my room with her on speaker phone and said, "Sharon listen to your crazy daughter she's psycho she just keeps crying, come get her!" My mom asked me what was wrong and I told her that granny had beaten me, and of course my grandmother denied it, and I began to wail. I needed a way out, and then my mom said, "Kourtney then you need to go to the insane floor at the hospital." I screamed for her to take me to save me. In my mind I knew I wanted to be anywhere but where I was at the time.

My grandmother got off the phone and she told me, you want to go to the insane hospital ok, if you don't stop I will give you a shock treatment like they do at the insane hospital, then she stormed off. I laid there and kept crying, feeling sorry for myself. Not too long afterwards my grandmother appears at my doorway this time with a big yellow flower pot full to the brim of ice cold water. She looked at me and said, "If you don't stop crying I'm going to give you a shock treatment." I tried with everything within me to stop crying because I knew that what she was saying was true.

Sadly, I took one second too long and she dumped a big flower pot of ice cold water all over me. I gasped in agony, the water was so cold, but as it hit me I became numb. I then made up in my mind that I wouldn't cry no more. I got up and cleaned up the water. My grandmother then insisted on perming my hair after she had just made it wet. I later finished washing my clothes and kept my mouth shut. I couldn't wait to get to school the next day. I knew that while I was at school I was safe.

I couldn't let anyone see me sad or hurting, so I kept the same smile on my face as I did every time things went awry in my life. When I got home I began to realize that I moved from one place of abuse to another place of abuse. I started going through the phone book and looked for homeless shelters, but my grandmother caught on to what I was doing.

She told me that if I thought that I was going to leave, I was sadly mistaken, and if I walked out of the house she said she would blow my brains out in her front yard. Covering up the incident by saying I was in her yard trespassing.

"Behold, I have given you the power to tread on snakes and scorpions, and upon every power of the enemy nothing will harm you!" -Luke 10:18-19

CHAPTER SIX
WAY OF ESCAPE

Two weeks after the incident between me and my grandmother, I was unexpectedly called into the guidance office. My counselor asked me what was going on. She had noticed a decline in my grades, at that moment; I cried out to her and told her what I was going through at home. I told her what my grandmother had done to me, and how I was always in fear and torment.

She started making phone calls to different people, and she got in contact with this women's abuse shelter. She told them my situation they instructed her that they would be sending a car to pick me up. I could stay there until I graduated from high school. With three months of school left, I was eager to get there. That day I never went home, and my grandmother came looking for me at the school, I watched her through the windows but I never came out. She drove off and a cab pulled up to take me to this unknown place.

When I pulled up to the street there was this big gate with surveillance cameras on it. The driver stated his name and they let him in. I didn't know what to expect when I got there. I went there with only the clothes on my back, and they signed me in and gave me a bed. The shelter happened to be in this big beautiful mansion, and it was full of broken-hearted and abused women; women who had lost everything but their dignity; women who didn't have any where else to turn to.

In the shelter, I would walk around and talk to each woman individually and listen to their stories. Some were abused by husbands, boyfriends, and girlfriends. I began to talk about the only person that I knew never left me and gave me comfort: God. While I lived in this shelter I met this woman with a daughter, she was on the run from her abusive husband.

Her daughter brought joy to me; she would walk around and sing songs to me that would bring smiles to my face. I never knew the degree of fear that a woman could experience. On this particular day she wanted to go to Wal-Mart. So we drove about an hour to the next town to go to Wal-Mart, in fear that her husband was going to see her. She put on a wig and we went in. The whole time we were there she looked over her shoulder, and kept her daughter and me close to her. Little did I know that was going to be the last day that I would ever see her again.

The next day when I got to school, the principal called me to the office, it turned out that my grandmother had come up to the school trying to sign me out. They were concerned about the welfare of my life so I stayed in the office and told him the story. I told him that I didn't have anything; no clothes and no shoes.

Mr. Davis reached in his pocket and gave me $100 and told me to go get some clothes when I got out of school. When I made it home that evening, the women were all gathered around hugging and crying. It turns out the woman who I had just spent time with, was gone. She had another woman drive her to a secret location to get a car and then she drove to Arizona.

It turned out that earlier that day her husband had come to the shelter with the Police department trying to take their child. The love of a mother is a powerful thing, and it caused her to leave for the safety of her child. That night I cried myself to sleep, my heart went out to her. I laid there wondering why good people had to go through such horrible things.

DIVINE INTERVENTION

Another one of my roommate's named Crystal asked me did I want to go to her new church that she was attending. I hadn't been to church in years and I had nothing else better to do, so I went. The ride to church was a quiet one and I didn't know what to expect. We pulled up to a small white church called Christ Temple Apostolic Church.

When I went in the building I was greeted with warm smiles and received genuine hugs. The sermon that was preached made me feel like the Pastor was talking directly to me. I knew then it was time to start serving God wholeheartedly. Sadly, I didn't go back after that one time while living in the shelter. Crystal wound up leaving and I didn't hear from her again, until later on.

I Love the Lord, because He hears My voice and my supplications. Because He has inclined His ear to me, Therefore I shall call upon Him as long as I live.
                              -Psalms 116:12

CHAPTER SEVEN

TRANSITION

The next day at school I met up with my friend Senchal.
I told her of every account of abuse I went through from the age
of 4 to 18. She sat there in astonishment. She couldn't believe
that I had gone through all those things. She reassured me that
things would get better, and she asked me to ride home with
her after school that day. When we got to her house she intro-
duced me to her mother and her step-father.

Not knowing what she had up her sleeve, Senchal asked
her mom if I could move in with them until I graduated from
high school. I was so use to rejection that I didn't expect to hear
her say yes. I didn't know what to say. On my way back to the
shelter I was thinking of ways to not hurt my new familys'
heart. I had come to a complacent place in my heart and reminded myself that this was the best decision so I could graduate.

"Until now you have not asked for anything in my name." Ask and you will receive, and your joy will be complete." -John 16:24

When I got there I told my counselor that I had found somewhere to go, and since I was 18 I didn't have to stay at the shelter anymore.

The experience at the shelter was something I would never forget. I had developed relationships with these women. We cried together, ate together, and encouraged each other. Besides our womanhood all we had was each other. I decided that I wouldn't tell everyone I was leaving. I wanted to leave as swiftly as possible. So Senchal, her mother, and I packed my stuff and put it in the car.

SENIOR PROM

With a month left till graduation Senchal talked me into going to my senior prom at the last minute. So many things had to be done. I had to rush to find a dress, the only formal dress I had was an old raggedy pink dress that I had wore to prom my sophomore year. Senchal looked in her closet she insisted that I wear the white dress she had worn to a pageant. When seeing the dress I was amazed. I thought it was the most beautiful thing that anyone had given to me. I've received lots of hand me downs throughout my life, but nothing that new. With my dress squared away the only thing left was to get a Prom date. I wasn't too big on asking people, and no one had made any hints that they were interested in going to the Prom with me.

While leaving school one day, I was walking across the courtyard and Senchal called my name. I went over to her to see what was up. When I walked up to her, standing next to her was two young guys Brandon and Dwayne. She told me that Brandon was a Sophomore and would love to take me to the Prom. To myself I thought man he short, and what I look like going to Prom with a Sophomore. This boy couldn't possibly show me a good time. Realizing I had no other choice but him I went along with it.

The next few days were pure hell. Senchal and I decided we would ride together with whoever her prom date was. Little to my surprise I found out that Senchal was actually going to prom with Bill, and once he found out we lived together he told her that I couldn't ride with them. I started to back out, but Brandon worked out the situation. He had a few friends who offered to let us ride with them.

This is not how my senior prom was supposed to turn out. I was supposed to be in Missouri enjoying my Prom with the friends I grew up with.

Despite the situation Brandon tried to make my Prom worth something. When the night finally came to an end, I made my way back home. I thanked Brandon for taking me to prom, and went into the house. He asked me did I want to hang out with them later on. I lied and told him I would call him later so we could hang out. I didn't want to go nowhere, I started feeling depressed once again. I started reflecting on my life everything that happened to me up until then. At many times I wanted to give up, but the vision of me graduating kept me moving forward. So many people had spoken against me achieving my diploma. I had to not only prove them wrong, but still prove myself right.

CHAPTER EIGHT
OVERCOMING THE ODDS

With graduation approaching in the next few days, I called my mom to see if she would be able to come. Her response was NO just as I thought it would be. Senchal's mother happened to had been standing by me when my mom said that. She took the phone from me and told her that after all the stuff I had been through she could at least make a point to come. She reminded her that it wasn't her obligation to care for me like I was her child, but she did it because she loved me. Not knowing if my mom would show up I prepared for graduation anyway.

It was a warm, Sunday evening; the grass smelled freshly cut, and the air smelled dense. As we lined up, in alphabetical order, I felt nothing but nerves and anxiousness. The valedictorians were giving their speeches, the choir sang, and the crowd applauded. It was finally time for the handing out of diplomas. So much was going through my mind. I was recalling all the times I cried, the struggle that led up to this day, the abuse and torment.

You always hear the testimonies that say I should have lost my mind...in a literal sense I almost lost my mind, but God kept it. They called the R's as I followed suit to the stage, my heart began to beat rapidly.

The principal called my name Kourtney Renee Ramsey, daughter of Bobby and Sharon Herron. I prayed daily for God to fix our relationship. I never thought the day would come that I would see them at my Senior Graduation. As I walked across the stage tears welled up in my eyes. I shook his hand, walked to the end of the stage and got my paper. Feeling very triumphant in my spirit I knew that all of the things I had endured had paid off. Knowing that God heard every cry, the long nights I sat up wondering if God truly heard me.

Most of the students looked at their diploma as the beginning of a new chapter in their life. Many had full rides to college but all I had was my dignity, sanity, and a smile. As I went back to my seat, and waited for everyone to get their diploma, the principal gave his closing remarks and it was time to switch the tassel and throw the hat.

Right before I threw my hat I brought all of the accounts of abuse from the first time I was sexually abused at the age of 4, being broken all the way down to no sense of emotion, and to living in a women's abuse shelter to the forefront of my mind. With tears streaming down my face, and my heart heavy from pain I threw my hat with everything in me. I felt a release, what was meant to break me empowered and encouraged me. When the Odds were against me God never left me, and he became my peace in the midst of the storm. God's grace is everlasting and his mercy is sufficient. God will always be glorified in my life. He held true to his promise: "I will never leave you nor forsake you."

EVERYTHING HAS ITS TIME

There is a time for everything,
and a season for every activity under heaven:
a time to be born and a time to die,
a time to plant and a time to uproot,
a time to kill and a time to heal,
a time to tear down and a time to build,
a time to weep and a time to laugh,
a time to mourn and a time to dance,
a time to scatter stones and a time to gather them,
a time to embrace and a time to refrain,
a time to search and a time to give up,
a time to keep and a time to throw away,
a time to tear and a time to mend,
a time to be silent and a time to speak,
a time to love and a time to hate,
a time for war and a time for peace.
Ecclesiastes 3:1-8

"Woe unto them that call evil good, and good evil; that put darkness for light, and light for darkness; that put bitter for sweet, and sweet for bitter!" -Isaiah 5:20

ABOUT THE AUTHOR

KOURTNEY RAMSEY began having dreams, visions, and hearing the voice of the Lord since the age of seven. She would use her to prophesy to family and friends. Along with the gift she experienced rejection which caused her to stop walking in her gift.

Throughout the course of her young life she experienced physical, emotional, and mental abuse. What was meant to break her became her strength. At the age of 18, she got baptized and filled with the fire of the holy-ghost. Because of the mishaps in her life, it has caused her to develop a deep passion for the youth.

Kourtney enjoys seeing the brokenhearted, misused, and abused set free through the love of Christ. She currently resides in Nashville, TN with her husband and two beautiful daughters.

Love is patient, love is kind. It does not envy,
it does not boast, it is not proud. It is not rude,
it is not self-seeking, it is not easily angered,
it keeps no record of wrongs. Love does not
delight in evil, but rejoices with the truth.
It always protects, always trusts,
always hopes, always perseveres.
-1 Corinthians 13:47

If we say that we have fellowship with Him, and walk in darkness, we lie and do not practice the truth.
-1 John 1:6

COMING SOON

Next Book: *Sleep'n with the Enemy:* Life after High School

THE MUSICIAN

"Tears streaming down my face, fingers going numb, Lord this is it, I think I'm going to die, I was gasping and squeezing his hand trying to get a release, then my sister runs in and jumps on him and starts hitting him, he released his grip off my throat. I choked and gasped for air, and cried silently to myself, while he wrestled and play fought my sister. I sat up on the bed, I knew if I took a run for it and went home, he would have chased me so I waited patiently for him to finish. He came in the room and said what's wrong with you? Why you crying I was just playing with you. I couldn't do nothing but look at him and cry. I was so distraught; I couldn't believe my ears at what he was saying to me..."

"There is no fear in love; but perfect love casteth out fear: because fear hath torment. He that feareth is not made perfect in love" -1John 4:18

NOTES

NOTES

To purchase copies of my book:
www.wix.com/prophetessk/pk

Thanks for your support
Kourtney Renee Ramsey

"And we know that in all things God works for good of those who love him,

who have been called according to his purpose." Romans 8:28

"Therefore I tell you, do not worry about your life, what you will eat or drink; or about your body, what you will wear. Is not life more important than food, and the body more important than clothes? Look at the birds of the air; they do not sow or reap or store away in barns, and yet your heavenly Father feeds them. Are you not much more valuable than they? Who of you by worrying can add a single hour to his life?

"And why do you worry about clothes? See how the lilies of the field grow. They do not labor or spin. Yet I tell you that not even Solomon in all his splendor was dressed like one of these. If that is how God clothes the grass of the field, which is here today and tomorrow is thrown into the fire, will he not much more clothe you, O you of little faith? So do not worry, saying, 'What shall we eat?' or 'What shall we drink?' or 'What shall we wear?' For the pagans run after all these things, and your heavenly Father knows that you need them. But seek first his kingdom and his righteousness, and all these things will be given to you as well.

-Matthew 6:25-33

"But seek first his kingdom and his righteousness, and all these things will be given to you as well."
-Matthew 6:33

OVERCOMING THE ODDS:
A YOUNG WOMAN'S STRUGGLES
TO STRENGTH

Kourtney Renee Greene